Second Letter
of St. Paul
to the Corinthians

Catholic Reflections
By
Giuseppe Scillia

DEDICATION

This book is dedicated to my wife and children. It is also dedicated to my parents without whom I would not exist. May the Lord bless them and keep them and bring them to eternal life.

Table of Contents

Second Letter of St. Paul to the Corinthians

Preface

The following reflections are not a work of systematic theology. This is not a scholarly work either. I will keep the references, quotes and sources to a minimum. My guiding principle will be to follow the biblical text as closely as possible, as it stands, limiting any reference to Catholic teachings as much as I can but fully aware of my Catholic worldview. My only claim will be to read the Scripture with basic common sense, in context, without preconceived ideas, as if I was reading St. Paul for the first time.

I have chosen the King James version of the text. One reason is that the it is in the public domain. The King James version is not necessary the best translation or the most accurate or the easiest to read but because it is a classic text of English literature, it seemed to me that it would be acceptable to everyone who wants to read the following reflections with an open mind. It is therefore a good standard and reference for the text.

I have divided this study in two main sections: reflections on the text itself and reflections on the themes. These are linked and build on each other but I thought it best to separate the two types of reflections in different sections. The main reason is that while commenting on the text, I did not want to write at length or I would fall into too many tangents and lose the train of thought that St. Paul follows.

In the reflections on the text, there are some verses I chose not to comment on because they seemed to me self-explanatory.

1

Instead I paraphrased the text to show St. Paul's continuity of thoughts. This is a complaint that many people often have about the way St. Paul writes. There are no breaks in his thought. A careful reading shows that these are the threads of the letter and I wanted to highlight this feature of his style of writing.

I could have analyzed this letter in every little detail, highlighting every word. Smarter people than me have done this. I refer the reader to the last 2000 years of commentaries, especially those by the early Fathers of the Church from the first century to the fifth (Ignatius of Antioch, Irenaeus of Lyons, John Chrysostom, Athanasius of Alexandria, Justin Martyr, Augustine of Hippo, Jerome of Jerusalem, etc.).

My hope is only to open the eyes of the reader in an ever so small way. To show Catholics where our doctrines come from and to give our Protestant brother and sisters enough curiosity to learn what Catholics really believe.

Introduction

In First Corinthians St. Paul is frustrated. You are not "once saved always saved" (1 Cor 10:12) Watch your actions, what you do has eternal consequences. God saved the Hebrews through the Red Sea but because of their sins he let them die in the desert; so it will be with you even if you think you are saved (1 Cor 10:2-5). You think you have received the Holy Spirit in the temple of your heart, but defile that temple and God will destroy you (1 Cor 3:16-17). Show reverence for the Eucharist or you will eat and drink damnation on yourself (1 Cor 11:29). In First Corinthians St. Paul is using tough love, he had to set them straight.

In Second Corinthians they are still proud, arrogant, presumptuous and divisive, but St. Paul changes the tone of his voice. The problem has not changed. The theology has not changed. The doctrine has not changed. This time the Corinthians don't need tough love anymore. St. Paul is hurt. The Corinthians are hurt. Sin hurts the faith. In this letter, St. Paul is showing them love and compassion and asks for love and compassion in return.

In some ways our Pope Francis is also misunderstood. Too many people think they see a change in the Catholic Church and hope that the teachings of the Church will change. Nothing is further from the truth. Pope Francis is not calling for a change in the teachings of the Church, he is calling for a change in our attitude with love and compassion for the sinner. St. Paul did not change his teaching on fornication and incest, nor did he change his teachings on the Eucharist, instead he asks for love and compassion for the sinners. Pope Francis is not asking for a change to the teachings on homosexuality or the Church stand on the reception of the Eucharist by divorced Catholics, instead he is asking for love and compassion for the sinners.

Some parts of the second letter to the Corinthians are difficult to follow because it refers to a previous letter. As far as chronology is concerned there seem to be four letters that St. Paul might have written to the Corinthians. One letter before the First Epistle and a third letter before the Second Epistle. Some scholars say that the first and the third letters are not lost but are included as part of our two canonical epistles. This is a subject that is for scholars to discuss. We don't need to do that. As far as our faith is concerned we accept the Canon of Scripture as it is written. It is inspired in all its parts, individually and in totality (Catechism of the Catholic Church #105). Another reason for not getting distracted by these scholarly discussions is that, if Scripture is the Living Word of God, then we must find the same eternal truths today as they were found in the past. There cannot be any new truths to be found but only a deeper understanding of the same truths that have been taught and passed on from the beginning (Galatians 1:8).

Just as an aside, St. Clement, the fourth pope, mentioned in Philippians 4:3, also had to write to the Corinthians. Again, the problem was division in the Church. The Corinthians still had not learned. But have we, in the 21st century learned? The Church is still divided by so many denominations and non-denominations. I know that it is often said that we must have unity in essentials and liberty in non essentials. But what is essential to the faith and who decides? Apparently Luther, Calvin, Zwingli, the Anglicans and the Anabaptists disagreed on many things and persecuted each other politically and religiously.

What is essential? Is baptism essential? Is the Eucharist essential? Is hierarchy essential? What is the place of works in salvation? If we have unity why are we separated? Do we take seriously what St. Paul says: *"There is one body, and one Spirit, even as ye are called in one hope of your calling; One Lord, one faith, one baptism"* (Ephesians 4:4-5)? We can only have one hope because there can only be one body/church under one Spirit. We can be united only by one God through one faith and one baptism. How can Quakers and Salvation Army deny baptism? How can Anglicans and Lutherans baptize infants and Baptists refuse if there is to be unity?

How can we proclaim we have the Truth to an unbelieving world if we cannot agree what the Truth is (John 17:20-23)? The divisions in our many churches and the many denominations and non-denominations, is a scandal to the faith and to the world.

Giuseppe Scillia

Reflections on the Text

Giuseppe Scillia

Chapter 1

As he did in First Corinthians, St. Paul has to re-establish his authority. He is an apostle by divine right. Like all letters he starts with salutations and blessings.

> *¹Paul, an apostle of Jesus Christ by the will of God, and Timothy our brother, unto the church of God which is at Corinth, with all the saints which are in all Achaia: ²Grace be to you and peace from God our Father, and from the Lord Jesus Christ. ³Blessed be God, even the Father of our Lord Jesus Christ, the Father of mercies, and the God of all comfort; ⁴Who comforteth us in all our tribulation, that we may be able to comfort them which are in any trouble, by the comfort wherewith we ourselves are comforted of God.*

St. Paul praises God, the Father of mercies and all comforts. Like in Romans and First Corinthians the focus is on the mercy of God. Even when we speak of the justice of God and our justification we are not talking of some kind of legal judgment and acquittal. We are talking of the mercy of God. Legal judgment might be passing of the law or passing of sentence. Legal judgment might be execution of the law but it is not justice. Justice is no justice if it does not have an element of mercy. The way the Father has shown mercy to us so we must show mercy to others.

> *⁵For as the sufferings of Christ abound in us, so our consolation also aboundeth by Christ. ⁶And whether we be afflicted, it is for your consolation and salvation, which is effectual in the enduring of the same sufferings which we also suffer: or whether we be comforted, it is for your consolation and salvation. ⁷And our hope of you is stedfast,*

2

knowing, that as ye are partakers of the sufferings, so shall ye be also of the consolation.

Paul is receiving a lot of sufferings like Christ but he also receives consolation in return. He knows that his sufferings are for the salvation of the Corinthians.

The mercy and consolation we show others is not just a nice thing to do. It's the core of our theology, our beliefs, and our faith. When we follow Jesus we identify with him. Christ suffered we suffer. He was afflicted we are afflicted. He consoles, we console. Suffering is part of our salvation and sanctification. Sometimes we don't know why we suffer but we can offer our suffering for the salvation of others, either by prayers or by offering it as a sacrifice for others. Our witness can be a powerful tool for evangelization. As others identify with our sufferings they can also identify with the consolation we have received from the Lord.

Similarly, St. Paul knows the sufferings that divisions have brought to the Corinthian church. He encourages them that, as they identify their sufferings with those of Christ, they will also experience consolation.

⁸For we would not, brethren, have you ignorant of our trouble which came to us in Asia, that we were pressed out of measure, above strength, insomuch that we despaired even of life: ⁹But we had the sentence of death in ourselves, that we should not trust in ourselves, but in God which raiseth the dead: ¹⁰Who delivered us from so great a death, and doth deliver: in whom we trust that he will yet deliver us; ¹¹Ye also helping together by prayer for us, that for the gift bestowed upon us by the means of many persons thanks may be given by many on our behalf.

This incident seems to be the one described in Acts 19:21-41. If it is then St. Paul had trouble in Ephesus and left the city because of the rioting he caused.

This is the kind of trouble where even life is in danger. In all our troubles we cannot rely on ourselves but we must rely on God who delivered us before and can deliver us again from all evil. We must always pray for one another. St. Paul is thanking those who have prayed for him.

> *12For our rejoicing is this, the testimony of our conscience, that in simplicity and godly sincerity, not with fleshly wisdom, but by the grace of God, we have had our conversation in the world, and more abundantly to you-ward. 13For we write none other things unto you, than what ye read or acknowledge; and I trust ye shall acknowledge even to the end; 14As also ye have acknowledged us in part, that we are your rejoicing, even as ye also are ours in the day of the Lord Jesus.*

St. Paul's conscience is clean. He has always acted with simplicity and sincerity with all but also especially with the Corinthians. What he is writing is exactly that, simple and sincere. What you read is what you get. He doesn't have any hidden agenda. He hopes they will understand and acknowledge this even to the end of time. The Corinthians are St. Paul's joy and he hopes that he is their joy.

> *15And in this confidence I was minded to come unto you before, that ye might have a second benefit; 16And to pass by you into Macedonia, and to come again out of Macedonia unto you, and of you to be brought on my way toward Judaea. 17When I therefore was thus minded, did I use lightness? or the things that I purpose, do I purpose according to the flesh, that with me there should be yea yea, and nay nay? 18But as God is true, our word toward you was not yea and nay. 19For the Son of God, Jesus Christ, who was preached among you by us, even by me and Silvanus and Timotheus, was not yea and nay, but in him was yea. 20For all the promises of God in him are yea, and in him Amen, unto the glory of God by us. 21Now he*

which stablisheth us with you in Christ, and hath anointed us, is God; [22]Who hath also sealed us, and given the earnest of the Spirit in our hearts.

St. Paul is so sure of their understanding that he wanted to visit the Corinthians again like he had said in his first letter (Ch. 4:18 and Ch. 16:3-9) but he was prevented of doing so. It is not his fault. When he speaks he is not making his plans according to worldly wisdom but according to the Lord's. It's not like he says yes one time and no another time. He did not change his mind. Like Jesus, the Son of God, who always says yes to the gift of salvation, Paul's intentions in preaching are always to say yes to the promises of God. His goal has always been the spiritual welfare of the Corinthians, to give them the promises of Christ. This is what he has been anointed to do.

[23]Moreover I call God for a record upon my soul, that to spare you I came not as yet unto Corinth. [24]Not for that we have dominion over your faith, but are helpers of your joy: for by faith ye stand.

St. Paul calls God as a witness that if he did not come to Corinth it is to spare them sorrow. He does not want to be a tyrannical leader of their faith. Rather he wants to lead them to joy and to be firm in their faith.

Chapter 2

St. Paul has made up his mind not to visit the Corinthians again. He doesn't want to cause pain to anyone.

> *¹But I determined this with myself, that I would not come again to you in heaviness. ²For if I make you sorry, who is he then that maketh me glad, but the same which is made sorry by me? ³And I wrote this same unto you, lest, when I came, I should have sorrow from them of whom I ought to rejoice; having confidence in you all, that my joy is the joy of you all. ⁴For out of much affliction and anguish of heart I wrote unto you with many tears; not that ye should be grieved, but that ye might know the love which I have more abundantly unto you. ⁵But if any have caused grief, he hath not grieved me, but in part: that I may not overcharge you all. ⁶Sufficient to such a man is this punishment, which was inflicted of many. ⁷So that contrariwise ye ought rather to forgive him, and comfort him, lest perhaps such a one should be swallowed up with overmuch sorrow.*

In the first epistle to the Corinthians we see them divided and forming groups around moral and doctrinal issues. Paul had to write to them with a heavy heart. Now he has resolved in his heart that he does not want to bring sorrow to the Corinthians. When he comes he wants to bring them joy as well as receive joy in return from them. He told them so in a previous letter, with tears and anguish because of the love he has for them. The one who has caused him pain has not done it to him but to all of them. This is punishment enough. It's time now to forgive and comfort him. St. Paul does not want anyone to grow in despair.

This is probably not the same person as in 1 Corinthians 5:3-5. Whether it is or whether it is a different person and a different problem, Paul's tone of voice has radically changed. Previously he recommended *"to deliver such an one unto Satan"* (excommunicate him). Even when speaking of excommunication we must remember it is not the same as shunning. Excommunication is to show the sinner that his sin separates him from God and from the community. Excommunication is supposed to be medicinal and redemptive in its purpose. Here instead, Paul recommends forgiveness and comfort.

The important message is that sometimes we need to apply tough love and sometimes mercy. In any case our goal is not to punish and destroy another person. Whichever we choose, our goal is to bring the sinner to salvation, an encounter with Christ, not to bring them to despair, swallowed up in sorrow.

> *[8]Wherefore I beseech you that ye would confirm your love toward him. [9]For to this end also did I write, that I might know the proof of you, whether ye be obedient in all things. [10]To whom ye forgive any thing, I forgive also: for if I forgave any thing, to whom I forgave it, for your sakes forgave I it in the person of Christ; [11]Lest Satan should get an advantage of us: for we are not ignorant of his devices*

The excommunication was a test for the sinner but it was also for the Corinthians to test their obedience to St. Paul. Now, enough is enough, this new command is not to contradict the first, it is to preserve unity and joy and see if the Corinthians will again obey St. Paul.

> *[12]Furthermore, when I came to Troas to preach Christ's gospel, and a door was opened unto me of the Lord, [13]I had no rest in my spirit, because I found not Titus my brother: but taking my leave of them, I went from thence into Macedonia. [14]Now thanks be unto God, which always causeth us to triumph in Christ, and maketh manifest the*

savour of his knowledge by us in every place. [15]For we are unto God a sweet savour of Christ, in them that are saved, and in them that perish: [16]To the one we are the savour of death unto death; and to the other the savour of life unto life. And who is sufficient for these things? [17]For we are not as many, which corrupt the word of God: but as of sincerity, but as of God, in the sight of God speak we in Christ.

At Troas a door was opened to preach the Gospel but St. Paul had to leave them to go to Macedonia. When preaching the Gospel St. Paul is always true to it, whether it will save some or whether it will convict others to spiritual death. He will not corrupt the word of God. He will speak it with sincerity in the sight of God, in Christ.

Chapter 3

St. Paul should not have to introduce himself. He founded the church in Corinth.

> *[1]Do we begin again to commend ourselves? or need we, as some others, epistles of commendation to you, or letters of commendation from you? [2]Ye are our epistle written in our hearts, known and read of all men: [3]Forasmuch as ye are manifestly declared to be the epistle of Christ ministered by us, written not with ink, but with the Spirit of the living God; not in tables of stone, but in fleshy tables of the heart.*

St. Paul does not need any letter of recommendation. His questions are rhetorical. The Corinthians are in his heart and he should be in theirs. Their life should be an open book to all. Their heart should be compassionate full of love not full of stubbornness. Their life should be the life of Christ full of the Holy Spirit.

> *[4]And such trust have we through Christ to God-ward: [5]Not that we are sufficient of ourselves to think any thing as of ourselves; but our sufficiency is of God; [6]Who also hath made us able ministers of the new testament; not of the letter, but of the spirit: for the letter killeth, but the spirit giveth life.*

The trust that St. Paul has is not in himself; it is the trust he has in Christ. He did not do anything. The faith of the Corinthians does not come from him, it comes from his call to minister the new covenant. St. Paul is contrasting the old covenant and the new; the covenant of the letter and the covenant of the spirit.

As he explained in the letter to the Romans (chapters 7 and 8) we have been freed from the Law (Ch 7:6). This has sometimes been misunderstood that we are free of all legal stipulations of the Old Testament. If that was true we would be free of the Ten Commandments. Would this mean that we can stop worshiping the One True God? Does it mean we can kill or commit adultery and still go to Heaven? God forbid.

It means that we are still bound by the Law (love of God and neighbors as the prophets taught – Matthew 22:37-40), but the Law should be in our heart (Deuteronomy 6:6) not just our lips. It is not the performance of the rules that will save us. The Law of God, the Law of Love, is not about tick the boxes on the checklist and getting brownie points for it. It's about living the Law with the mind of God. Loving with the heart of God. It is being transformed by the Holy Spirit. It is life giving because we seek a personal relationship with God.

> *7But if the ministration of death, written and engraven in stones, was glorious, so that the children of Israel could not stedfastly behold the face of Moses for the glory of his countenance; which glory was to be done away: 8How shall not the ministration of the spirit be rather glorious? 9For if the ministration of condemnation be glory, much more doth the ministration of righteousness exceed in glory. 10For even that which was made glorious had no glory in this respect, by reason of the glory that excelleth. 11For if that which is done away was glorious, much more that which remaineth is glorious.*

Christianity is like the Jewish religion grown up. As children we were given rules to follow. The rules were useful and we needed those rules but we were not able to truly live them. As adults we don't need the rules as a check list of things to do but thanks to the Holy Spirit the rules are not rules anymore they are part of who we are, they are life. If we consider the covenant with Israel and how glorious it was, how much more glorious is the covenant of the Gospel.

The covenant of the Jewish people, written in stone, was meant to be superseded. If the glory of the Law that Moses received was only a shadow of the real glory of the New Covenant (Hebrew 10:1). How much more glorious is this reality compared to the shadow.

> [12]*Seeing then that we have such hope, we use great plainness of speech:* [13]*And not as Moses, which put a vail over his face, that the children of Israel could not stedfastly look to the end of that which is abolished:* [14]*But their minds were blinded: for until this day remaineth the same vail untaken away in the reading of the old testament; which vail is done away in Christ.* [15]*But even unto this day, when Moses is read, the vail is upon their heart.* [16]*Nevertheless when it shall turn to the Lord, the vail shall be taken away.* [17]*Now the Lord is that Spirit: and where the Spirit of the Lord is, there is liberty.* [18]*But we all, with open face beholding as in a glass the glory of the Lord, are changed into the same image from glory to glory, even as by the Spirit of the Lord.*

This is our great hope we don't need to use figurative language, says St. Paul, we use as plain a language as we can. The children of Israel could not understand the Law. Their minds were blinded, even so today. But now the veil that prevented them to understand is being removed in Christ. In other words when we turn to the Lord, we are being made free. We are being changed into the image of God by the Spirit of God. It is as if we were gazing and contemplating in a mirror the glory of God.

Chapter 4

¹Therefore seeing we have this ministry, as we have received mercy, we faint not; ²But have renounced the hidden things of dishonesty, not walking in craftiness, nor handling the word of God deceitfully; but by manifestation of the truth commending ourselves to every man's conscience in the sight of God. ³But if our gospel be hid, it is hid to them that are lost: ⁴In whom the god of this world hath blinded the minds of them which believe not, lest the light of the glorious gospel of Christ, who is the image of God, should shine unto them.

The difference between the Old Testament and the New Testament is the ministry, the service for which Moses was anointed and the service for which Paul has been anointed. It is by the mercy of God that St. Paul has this ministry; therefore he does not lose hope. When St. Paul says that he is not acting this or that way, we get the sense that this is the problem he is facing again in Corinth. Those he is criticizing are using the Scriptures to teach false teachings with dishonesty, craftiness and deceit. On the contrary he, St. Paul, has received his New Testament ministry from God, he uses the plain truth of the Gospel and if anything he says seems obscure or absurd, it is not because of him or because of the Gospel but because people are blind to the truth and corrupt by the culture.

⁵For we preach not ourselves, but Christ Jesus the Lord; and ourselves your servants for Jesus' sake. ⁶For God, who commanded the light to shine out of darkness, hath shined in our hearts, to give the light of the knowledge of the glory of God in the face of Jesus Christ.

What's different about St. Paul? He does not use Scriptures for his own benefit but to preach Christ; the difference is his servant heart. He only teaches the truth and knowledge he has received, the knowledge of the glory of God. Jesus Christ is the face of the glory of God.

> *[7]But we have this treasure in earthen vessels, that the excellency of the power may be of God, and not of us. [8]We are troubled on every side, yet not distressed; we are perplexed, but not in despair; [9]Persecuted, but not forsaken; cast down, but not destroyed; [10]Always bearing about in the body the dying of the Lord Jesus, that the life also of Jesus might be made manifest in our body. [11]For we which live are alway delivered unto death for Jesus' sake, that the life also of Jesus might be made manifest in our mortal flesh. [12]So then death worketh in us, but life in you.*

This knowledge that St. Paul has is in him is like in a jar of clay, he has no power himself. The power of the knowledge he has comes only from God. Contrary to the others teachers who have acquired power through false teaching, all that St. Paul receives is troubles on every side. He does not feel despair, because whatever persecution he endures it is to manifest the life of Jesus. These persecutions, this death he suffers is for their sake, for the sake of the Corinthians eternal life.

> *[13]We having the same spirit of faith, according as it is written, I believed, and therefore have I spoken; we also believe, and therefore speak; [14]Knowing that he which raised up the Lord Jesus shall raise up us also by Jesus, and shall present us with you. [15]For all things are for your sakes, that the abundant grace might through the thanksgiving of many redound to the glory of God.*

St. Paul recalls psalm 116:10-14. The psalm describes the pains and sorrows of David, his calling on the Lord for deliverance, his faith in salvation, his partaking of sacramental wine, confessing his servant heart and salvation in the Lord. St. Paul preaches what he believes and this has brought him troubles on every side. But like David, he knows that his sufferings are temporary and that God will rescue him because he who raised Jesus will also raise us. These sufferings are for the Corinthians' sake and for God's glory.

> *[16]For which cause we faint not; but though our outward man perish, yet the inward man is renewed day by day. [17]For our light affliction, which is but for a moment, worketh for us a far more exceeding and eternal weight of glory; [18]While we look not at the things which are seen, but at the things which are not seen: for the things which are seen are temporal; but the things which are not seen are eternal.*

St. Paul does not lose heart. Even if our bodies are wasting away our spirit is being renewed day after day. These sorrows and afflictions that we suffer now are only for a moment and prepare us for our eternal glory.

Suffering, whether it is physical, emotional, mental or spiritual, is a serious matter and is not to be taken lightly. Sometimes we don't see the end of our sufferings and we complain to God. This is okay, David complained to God (psalm 13); even the saints in heaven complain to God (Revelation 6:10); even Jesus did (Matthew 27:46; psalm 22). God understands as long as we fix our eyes on what is unseen and is eternal (Philippians 3:14).

Chapter 5

¹For we know that if our earthly house of this tabernacle were dissolved, we have a building of God, an house not made with hands, eternal in the heavens. ²For in this we groan, earnestly desiring to be clothed upon with our house which is from heaven: ³If so be that being clothed we shall not be found naked. ⁴For we that are in this tabernacle do groan, being burdened: not for that we would be unclothed, but clothed upon, that mortality might be swallowed up of life. ⁵Now he that hath wrought us for the selfsame thing is God, who also hath given unto us the earnest of the Spirit.

We, Christians are in a strange situation. We live on this earth but we know that we don't belong here. Our soul is divided between two destinies. St. Paul uses some strange language for our twenty first century ears. When he speaks of house or building he speaks of our bodies and life. He is also contrasting life on earth with life in heaven, mortal life with eternal life. He says, we know that if our mortal life on earth was over then we would have our eternal life in heaven (verse 1). Here we suffer awaiting our life in heaven (verse 2) to finally receive eternal life (verse 3). In our mortal life we suffer and we groan. Not that we should be delivered from this life and die but that on the contrary, our death might bring us eternal (verse 4). For this reason God has given us the Holy Spirit as a pledge (verse 5).

The idea that St. Paul is teaching is that our bodies are mortal and subject to suffering and death. We all hope that this will end someday, that we should not die or suffer anymore. Now God has already given us eternal life today but it is not complete yet until we finally reach heaven. That's why we have this dual destiny pulling us apart between our current life, even when it is suffering, and the eternal life that we have been promised and that we have already entered by virtue of our baptism. The Holy Spirit is that promise.

> *⁶Therefore we are always confident, knowing that, whilst we are at home in the body, we are absent from the Lord: ⁷(For we walk by faith, not by sight:) ⁸We are confident, I say, and willing rather to be absent from the body, and to be present with the Lord. ⁹Wherefore we labour, that, whether present or absent, we may be accepted of him. ¹⁰For we must all appear before the judgment seat of Christ; that every one may receive the things done in his body, according to that he hath done, whether it be good or bad.*

This gives us confidence even though we know that as long as we live here we are away from the full presence of God. We are confident because we walk by faith not by sight, we are able to suffer because we know that eternal life awaits us and we trust those things that are unseen because they are eternal (Ch. 4:18). Therefore we try to please the Lord because we will all be judge for the things we have done in this body in our life, for the good or the evil we have done.

The two doctrines that St. Paul is teaching us here are that we have already eternal life here and now, even though we are still subject to suffering and death. We need to rely, not on our senses, but on our faith to understand this. The second teaching follows from the first, because we know we have already entered eternal life here and now, we must live it as we were already in heaven, pleasing God, knowing that we will be judged according to our works, whether good or evil. Too many people think that works have nothing to do with our salvation but Christianity is a religion that makes moral demands on us in this body in this life because Christianity is an incarnate religion. It is not just our souls that have been redeemed but our bodies as well. What we do in our bodies has eternal consequences (1 Corinthians 6:9) and we will be judged accordingly.

> *[11]Knowing therefore the terror of the Lord, we persuade men; but we are made manifest unto God; and I trust also are made manifest in your consciences. [12]For we commend not ourselves again unto you, but give you occasion to glory on our behalf, that ye may have somewhat to answer them which glory in appearance, and not in heart. [13]For whether we be beside ourselves, it is to God: or whether we be sober, it is for your cause. [14]For the love of Christ constraineth us; because we thus judge, that if one died for all, then were all dead: [15]And that he died for all, that they which live should not henceforth live unto themselves, but unto him which died for them, and rose again.*

St. Paul wants to be as transparent as possible. Because he knows the fear of the Lord, he is preaching to others, being as honestly open in the eyes of God as well as in the eyes of the Corinthians. His goal is not to be commended for what he does but to be an example to them against does who rely on the appearance of faith rather than the faith that comes from the heart. If he sounds crazy it is for God; if he sounds rational it is for the Corinthians. It is the love of God that drives him; Christ died for all that all might die to the world and no longer live for themselves but live for Christ who redeemed them.

> *[16]Wherefore henceforth know we no man after the flesh: yea, though we have known Christ after the flesh, yet now henceforth know we him no more. [17]Therefore if any man be in Christ, he is a new creature: old things are passed away; behold, all things are become new. [18]And all things are of God, who hath reconciled us to himself by Jesus Christ, and hath given to us the ministry of reconciliation; [19]To wit, that God was in Christ, reconciling the world unto himself, not imputing their trespasses unto them; and hath*

committed unto us the word of reconciliation. ²⁰Now then *we are ambassadors for Christ, as though God did beseech* *you by us: we pray you in Christ's stead, be ye reconciled* *to God. ²¹For he hath made him to be sin for us, who knew* *no sin; that we might be made the righteousness of God in* *him.*

Anyone who is in Christ is a new creation, the old has passed away, and the new has come. This God has done and has reconciled us to himself through Christ, not counting our sins against us. For this he has given us the ministry of reconciliation. Now we are ambassadors for Christ as if God pleaded through us. We beg you to be reconciled with God for he made Christ to bear our sins so that we may be made holy in him.

Some Christians think that verse 21 means that Christ became sin and he had to be sacrificed to God the Father because God the Father cannot stand sin. This violates the doctrine of the Trinity, there are three divine persons but only one God, which means the Father's mission is Christ's mission and the Spirit's mission (John 10:30-38 and John 14:9), it also means that God (the Father) cannot kill God (the Son). This violates the doctrine of Christ's divinity, Jesus is the second person of the Trinity, and therefore Jesus is divine and cannot sin (Hebrews 4:15). This violates the sovereignty of Christ who gives his life of his own will (John 10:18). Verse 21 is simply a figurative way of saying Christ bore our sins so that we may be reconciled with God.

Chapter 6

Salvation is cooperation with God's will.

> *¹We then, as workers together with him, beseech you also that ye receive not the grace of God in vain. ²(For he saith, I have heard thee in a time accepted, and in the day of salvation have I succoured thee: behold, now is the accepted time; behold, now is the day of salvation.)*

Whether it is our own salvation where we cooperate with God's will in our life or whether we go out witnessing to those around us we work together with him, we are his coworkers. This is even more so for an ordained minister like St. Paul. This realization becomes very urgent and compels him to beg the Corinthians who are in danger of losing their salvation. God has done his part, he has helped them (redeemed them), but they have to accept salvation now not later. When God gives us his grace we should not delay to accept it.

This is a good verse to remember when some people calling themselves followers of Jesus claim to be saved and born again but on the other hand they delay receiving baptism. Following Christ means doing what he says and does. When he says that those who believe and are baptized will be saved (Mark 16:16), it means you must be baptized now. Peter says the same thing (Acts 2:38) and so did Paul (Acts 9:18). Now is the day of salvation, not later. When God gives us his grace, baptism and other graces, let's obey and accept his will immediately.

> *³Giving no offence in any thing, that the ministry be not blamed: ⁴But in all things approving ourselves as the*

ministers of God, in much patience, in afflictions, in necessities, in distresses, ⁵In stripes, in imprisonments, in tumults, in labours, in watchings, in fastings; ⁶By pureness, by knowledge, by longsuffering, by kindness, by the Holy Ghost, by love unfeigned, ⁷By the word of truth, by the power of God, by the armour of righteousness on the right hand and on the left, ⁸By honour and dishonour, by evil report and good report: as deceivers, and yet true; ⁹As unknown, and yet well known; as dying, and, behold, we live; as chastened, and not killed; ¹⁰As sorrowful, yet alway rejoicing; as poor, yet making many rich; as having nothing, and yet possessing all things.

St. Paul does not do anything that might give a bad name to his ministry of reconciliation. On the contrary his ministry is about patience and hardship, persecutions and fasting, kindness and holiness, love and truth. His only defense is justice, given everywhere left and right. Whether honored or dishonored, praised or bad mouthed, always true, well known or unknown, dying or punished he is alive, himself being poor making many spiritually rich, he, St. Paul, does not have anything and yet he has been richly blessed by God.

¹¹O ye Corinthians, our mouth is open unto you, our heart is enlarged. ¹²Ye are not straitened in us, but ye are straitened in your own bowels. ¹³Now for a recompence in the same, (I speak as unto my children,) be ye also enlarged.

St. Paul has been frank and his heart is wide open by the love he has for the Corinthians. He asks them to do the same, and not be entangled by their passions.

¹⁴Be ye not unequally yoked together with unbelievers: for what fellowship hath righteousness with unrighteousness? and what communion hath light with darkness? ¹⁵And what concord hath Christ with Belial? or what part hath he that believeth with an infidel?

These are some of the same problems that St. Paul addressed in his First Letter to the Corinthians. They still struggle with the same issues: partnership with unbelievers, either in marriage or fellowship (1 Cor. 7:14), partaking into pagan sacrifices (1 Cor. 10:20), and their temples (1 Cor. 3:16-18).

> *16And what agreement hath the temple of God with idols? for ye are the temple of the living God; as God hath said, I will dwell in them, and walk in them; and I will be their God, and they shall be my people. 17Wherefore come out from among them, and be ye separate, saith the Lord, and touch not the unclean thing; and I will receive you, 18And will be a Father unto you, and ye shall be my sons and daughters, saith the Lord Almighty.*

We belong to God not to idols. We are his people and therefore we need to keep ourselves apart from all unclean things. We are his temple. Sometimes we read verses like these and we give them a figurative meaning. But for St. Paul the temple of God is not a figure of speech. He is not talking of God as being in our hearts. St. Paul uses this kind of phrase literally, that's why in 1 Corinthians 3:16-17, he can be so abrupt and threatening, "you defile the Temple and God will destroy you." This personal threat did happen to the actual Temple that God destroyed on August 10, AD 70.

The Temple is where God meets man. By extension the Garden of Eden is represented as a temple; it is not by chance that the description of creation ends on the Sabbath day when man is to rest with God (Genesis 2:3). This is throughout Scriptures whether it is the building of the Tabernacle (Exodus 25:8-9 and Hebrew 8:5) or the incarnation (John 1:14). This is also apparent in the book of Revelation when St. John has a vision of Heaven (Revelation 4:1) or when he describes the New Jerusalem (Revelation 22:1-3).

The point is that our soul, our own being, our own body, is truly where God dwells, the meeting place of God and man. This is not a metaphor. This is not figurative language. This is the certain truth of the faith. This, the Spirit indwelling our soul, it is just as true as the genes of our parents indwelling our body.

When Christians think of the cross as the finished work of Christ and accepting his sacrifice as the ultimate sign of our salvation, it is true but it leaves out our destiny. What are we saved for? What does it look like? How do we get there? The indwelling of the Holy Spirit is what sanctifies us to make us ready for heaven (Revelation 20:27). It is what makes us children of God, heir to everything that Christ has, the love of the Trinity (Romans 8:15-17).

We cannot achieve this kind of salvation without sanctification, without holiness, without the Holy Spirit. By this we are divinized by adoption not by nature (theosis). This is our ultimate destiny. Therefore let's keep ourselves clean of sins and God will receive us as his children (verses 17 and 18).

Chapter 7

¹Having therefore these promises, dearly beloved, let us cleanse ourselves from all filthiness of the flesh and spirit, perfecting holiness in the fear of God.

Christ shared our humanity so that we may share in his divinity. This is also what St. Peter teaches. The promise we have received is that we will share in the divine nature (2 Peter 1:4), but we must add virtue to our faith (verse 5) if we want to keep our salvation (verse 10). We must clean ourselves from physical and spiritual filth. We are not just saved but we are saved to be holy.

²Receive us; we have wronged no man, we have corrupted no man, we have defrauded no man. ³I speak not this to condemn you: for I have said before, that ye are in our hearts to die and live with you. ⁴Great is my boldness of speech toward you, great is my glorying of you: I am filled with comfort, I am exceeding joyful in all our tribulation.

St. Paul wants to be accepted by the Corinthians. He does not want to condemn them. They are in his heart; their destiny is joined together with his. Despite the difficulties he has hope and joy in them.

⁵For, when we were come into Macedonia, our flesh had no rest, but we were troubled on every side; without were fightings, within were fears. ⁶Nevertheless God, that comforteth those that are cast down, comforted us by the coming of Titus; ⁷And not by his coming only, but by the consolation wherewith he was comforted in you, when he told us your earnest desire, your mourning, your fervent mind toward me; so that I rejoiced the more. [8]For though I made you sorry with a letter, I do not repent, though I did repent: for I perceive that the same epistle hath made you sorry, though it were but for a season. [9]Now I rejoice, not that ye were made sorry, but that ye sorrowed to repentance: for ye were made sorry after a godly manner, that ye might receive damage by us in nothing.

St. Paul has had his share of troubles since he went to Macedonia but the comfort that the Corinthians gave Titus has given St. Paul comfort as well. The letter he sent them made them sorry, not to despair but to repent. Sometimes we must use tough love. It might be unpleasant to the children and it is unpleasant to the parents as well. The purpose is not to make someone sorry but to provoke a change into a godly attitude.

[10]For godly sorrow worketh repentance to salvation not to be repented of: but the sorrow of the world worketh death. [11]For behold this selfsame thing, that ye sorrowed after a godly sort, what carefulness it wrought in you, yea, what clearing of yourselves, yea, what indignation, yea, what fear, yea, what vehement desire, yea, what zeal, yea, what revenge! In all things ye have approved yourselves to be clear in this matter. [12]Wherefore, though I wrote unto you, I did it not for his cause that had done the wrong, nor for his cause that suffered wrong, but that our care for you in the sight of God might appear unto you.

This is also a psychological truth. It's not enough to be sorry; you have to want to change. Being sorry brings no fruit except sorrow, despair and death, either the death of a person or the death of a relationship. Being sorry is only the first step, to be fruitful and life giving it must bring change. If we do something wrong we don't say "I am sorry" but say "I am sorry and I resolve not to do it again with God's help." This act of contrition clears us of wrong doing, it absolves us. This zeal to change is what really shows how much the Corinthians care for St. Paul.

13Therefore we were comforted in your comfort: yea, and exceedingly the more joyed we are for the joy of Titus, because his spirit was refreshed by you all. 14For if I have boasted anything to him of you, I am not ashamed; but as we spake all things to you in truth, even so our boasting, which I made before Titus, is found a truth. 15And his inward affection is more abundant toward you, whilst he remembereth the obedience of you all, how with fear and trembling ye received him. 16I rejoice therefore that I have confidence in you in all things.

This is real comfort; St. Paul is comforted because the Corinthians have been comforted, even more so because the joy of Titus gives him joy. A father is always comforted by the joy of his children. This repentance makes true everything positive that St. Paul said to Titus. This boasting, this pride, this bragging all came true. This obedience of the Corinthians gives St. Paul and Titus even greater affection and confidence in them.

In all of this the Corinthians show the filial fear of Titus and St. Paul that we usually associate with God, the fear to hurt a loved one. In the fear and trembling they had when receiving Titus we see the role of the Church hierarchy and the obedience we owe our leaders. This is not a dictatorial hierarchy but a familial one where the goal is not power and slavery but love and compassion (Hebrews 13:17).

Chapter 8

¹Moreover, brethren, we do you to wit of the grace of God bestowed on the churches of Macedonia; ²How that in a great trial of affliction the abundance of their joy and their deep poverty abounded unto the riches of their liberality. ³For to their power, I bear record, yea, and beyond their power they were willing of themselves; ⁴Praying us with much intreaty that we would receive the gift, and take upon us the fellowship of the ministering to the saints. ⁵And this they did, not as we hoped, but first gave their own selves to the Lord, and unto us by the will of God. ⁶Insomuch that we desired Titus, that as he had begun, so he would also finish in you the same grace also. ⁷Therefore, as ye abound in everything, in faith, and utterance, and knowledge, and in all diligence, and in your love to us, see that ye abound in this grace also.

We are not just saved but we are saved to be holy. Love and compassion is our destiny. And it starts here and now. The churches of Macedonia are a good example of generosity. Despite afflictions and poverty they still found the joy of giving. St. Paul might be referring to the collection he talked about in his first epistle to the Corinthians (chapter 16). If this is the case, St. Paul wanted to go to Corinth to correct their doctrinal and discipline errors. He also wanted to take up a collection for the Church in Jerusalem (maybe famine or persecution). He is using their generosity as an example of Christian giving to illustrate the point he has been making throughout the letter.

Love and compassion are the trademark of a Christian. Comforting others in their afflictions, whatever the affliction, is our purpose in life. We show others the love that God gave us first (1 John 4:19). This is what we Catholics call the works of mercy. St. Paul is only repeating what Jesus said his mission was (Luke 4:18-19), what he taught in the Sermon on the Mount (Matthew chapter 5), and what judgment will be based on (Matthew 25:41-43). If faith is what saves us why is it that showing mercy is a test for salvation? Because as Jesus said:

"Thou shalt love the Lord thy God with all thy heart, and with all thy soul, and with all thy mind. This is the first and great commandment. And the second is like unto it, Thou shalt love thy neighbour as thyself. On these two commandments hang all the law and the prophets (Matthew 22:36-40)."

Love of God is the first part of the Ten Commandments; love of neighbor is the second part. Love of God and neighbor are the two sides of the same coin, we cannot have one without the other. We cannot love God whom we have not seen without loving first our neighbor whom we see (John 4:20).

As Christians we don't give the first fruits or a tenth of our wealth. We give it all because it all belongs to God. A tenth becomes an obligation; giving it all, giving of oneself comes from joy. Someone said the gifts we are given were never meant for us but to give back to others, we are not the recipient of the gifts but the conduit, the instrument of God's mercy.

The Macedonians who had nothing gave all with joy. St. Paul asks the Corinthians, who have everything, to show their love for him by how much grace they receive in giving.

⁸I speak not by commandment, but by occasion of the forwardness of others, and to prove the sincerity of your love. ⁹For ye know the grace of our Lord Jesus Christ, that, though he was rich, yet for your sakes he became poor, that ye through his poverty might be rich. ¹⁰And herein I give my advice: for this is expedient for you, who have begun before, not only to do, but also to be forward a year ago. [11]Now therefore perform the doing of it; that as there was a readiness to will, so there may be a performance also out of that which ye have. [12]For if there be first a willing mind, it is accepted according to that a man hath, and not according to that he hath not. [13]For I mean not that other men be eased, and ye burdened: [14]But by an equality, that now at this time your abundance may be a supply for their want, that their abundance also may be a supply for your want: that there may be equality: [15]As it is written, He that had gathered much had nothing over; and he that had gathered little had no lack.

St. Paul does not command the Corinthians but he asks them to show that this comes from their heart just as Christ did who made himself poor (God who became a man) so that we may become rich (receive his divinity by adoption).

He asks this not as a command but to complete what they promised. He wants them to give but not to overburden themselves. He is only asking for fairness, to supply for the needs of others. When we supply others with financial help out of our abundance, we will receive out of their abundance what we need in return. Those who lack financial wealth many times have spiritual wealth. It is not the amount of money that we give, it is the heart and love with which we give that will increase our spiritual wealth. The point is not to redistribute wealth in equal amounts as if we all had the same needs. Equality is rather a matter of solidarity among the rich and the poor. St. Paul is not speaking of political and social equality. He is speaking of solidarity among members of the same family, the children of God.

[16]But thanks be to God, which put the same earnest care into the heart of Titus for you. [17]For indeed he accepted the exhortation; but being more forward, of his own accord he went unto you. [18]And we have sent with him the brother,

whose praise is in the gospel throughout all the churches;
[19]And not that only, but who was also chosen of the
churches to travel with us with this grace, which is
administered by us to the glory of the same Lord, and
declaration of your ready mind: [20]Avoiding this, that no
man should blame us in this abundance which is
administered by us: [21]Providing for honest things, not only
in the sight of the Lord, but also in the sight of men. [22]And
we have sent with them our brother, whom we have
oftentimes proved diligent in many things, but now much
more diligent, upon the great confidence which I have in
you. [23]Whether any do enquire of Titus, he is my partner
and fellow helper concerning you: or our brethren be
enquired of, they are the messengers of the churches, and
the glory of Christ. [24]Wherefore shew ye to them, and
before the churches, the proof of your love, and of our
boasting on your behalf.

It is the same care and love that Titus has for them, who went to visit them of his initiative. St. Paul recommends Titus as having been anointed for this mission and he asks the Corinthians to show their love for him and to give generously.

Chapter 9

¹For as touching the ministering to the saints, it is superfluous for me to write to you: ²For I know the forwardness of your mind, for which I boast of you to them of Macedonia, that Achaia was ready a year ago; and your zeal hath provoked very many. ³Yet have I sent the brethren, lest our boasting of you should be in vain in this behalf; that, as I said, ye may be ready: ⁴Lest haply if they of Macedonia come with me, and find you unprepared, we (that we say not, ye) should be ashamed in this same confident boasting. ⁵Therefore I thought it necessary to exhort the brethren, that they would go before unto you, and make up beforehand your bounty, whereof ye had notice before, that the same might be ready, as a matter of bounty, and not as of covetousness.

St. Paul is trying to spur the Corinthians to give some money for the help of the Church in Jerusalem. He is gently pitting them in a friendly competition with the Macedonians. He seems to say I told them about your generosity; don't disappoint me. St. Paul is sending some brothers in Christ to prepare in advance the Corinthians' gifts, so that when they give it will be out of their heart and not out of obligation.

Notice how St. Paul is now using the singular first person pronoun "I" unlike before when he has been using the pronoun "we."

⁶But this I say, He which soweth sparingly shall reap also sparingly; and he which soweth bountifully shall reap also bountifully. ⁷Every man according as he purposeth in his heart, so let him give; not grudgingly, or of necessity: for God loveth a cheerful giver. [8]And God is able to make all grace abound toward you; that ye, always having all sufficiency in all things, may abound to every good work: [9](As it is written, He hath dispersed abroad; he hath given to the poor: his righteousness remaineth for ever.

He who sows sparingly will reap sparingly. God loves a cheerful giver and will give him abundant grace.

This could sound like the health and wealth gospel of television preachers. Those preachers teach that when you give (sow your seed) God is under an obligation to bless you with prosperity. It's a tic for tac theology. It is the erroneous theology of the Pharisees. It is trying to manipulate God with the New Age deception of the law of reciprocity.

Christian giving has nothing to do with manipulating God. It is about giving from the heart. It is about doing those good works that the Holy Spirit has prepared for us to do (Ephesians 2:10). As Jesus explains, with these we will inherit eternal life (Matthew 24:34-40). These will make us righteous for ever (verse 9). Christian giving is not about self-seeking prosperity. Christian giving is about love of neighbor. Out of love for our neighbor we give and God in return out of his love he will give us more spiritual grace. Giving is not material redistribution of wealth it is a spiritual act of love. Without counting we give of our material gifts, without counting God will gives us grace.

[10]Now he that ministereth seed to the sower both minister bread for your food, and multiply your seed sown, and increase the fruits of your righteousness; [11]Being enriched in every thing to all bountifulness, which causeth through us thanksgiving to God. [12]For the administration of this service not only supplieth the want of the saints, but is abundant also by many thanksgivings unto God; [13]Whiles by the experiment of this ministration they glorify God for

your professed subjection into the gospel of Christ, and for your liberal distribution unto them, and unto all men; [14]And by their prayer for you, which long after you for the exceeding grace of God in you. [15]Thanks be unto God for his unspeakable gift.

God who supplies seed for those who sow will also provide for our financial and spiritual needs. Being enriched in all things we can only give more thanksgiving to God. Seed, bread, bounty, thanksgiving reminds us that all we have, material and spiritual, comes from God and that the only return we can make to God is an abundant return of thanksgiving (seed, bread, thanksgiving, Eucharist).

The whole gist of this passage is that it is in giving that we receive. As brothers in Christ we are all one family. We are all interconnected like the different parts of a body (1 Corinthians, chapter 12). When one of us suffers we all suffer. When one of us receives joy we all receive joy. Giving to others is giving thanks to God for what he has given us, which then produces joy and prayers which will bring us back even more grace. This in itself is a blessing from God to both the one who gives and the one who receives.

Chapter 10

¹Now I Paul myself beseech you by the meekness and gentleness of Christ, who in presence am base among you, but being absent am bold toward you: ²But I beseech you, that I may not be bold when I am present with that confidence, wherewith I think to be bold against some, which think of us as if we walked according to the flesh. ³For though we walk in the flesh, we do not war after the flesh: ⁴(For the weapons of our warfare are not carnal, but mighty through God to the pulling down of strong holds;) ⁵Casting down imaginations, and every high thing that exalteth itself against the knowledge of God, and bringing into captivity every thought to the obedience of Christ; ⁶And having in a readiness to revenge all disobedience, when your obedience is fulfilled.

I beg you by the humility and gentleness of Christ. I beg you so that I may not have to show you my power as I will have to show against those who think I am living and preaching out of worldly pride. Yes, we are in the world and have to deal with worldly affairs but our weapons are not of this world, they are the weapons of the power of God. We are ready to punish anyone who disobey us.

St. Paul is still struggling with his need to affirm doctrine and his need to comfort and encourage the Corinthians. This is a fine balance to achieve. In the preceding chapters St. Paul has tried to encourage the Corinthians by using some form of friendly spiritual competition between the attitude of the Macedonians and the Corinthians. But they still have among them some people who deny St. Paul's authority. This was obvious in the First Letter. Here he is trying to be more friendly. He is still reinforcing the doctrine of interdependence in the body of Christ and the need to provide charity for the needs of the Church in Jerusalem but the opposition he encounters from some people is still there.

We see this as he starts using the pronoun "I" in the first verse. Then in the middle of the second verse he switches to the pronoun "we." When he speaks of meekness and gentleness as his personal imitation of Christ he uses "I." When he speaks of those who accuse him of worldly pride and who are disobedient to his teaching, then suddenly, in the middle of the sentence he use "us" and "we." The "we" indicates St. Paul's authority as an Apostle which is being opposed, and when he is being opposed he will reinforce his divinely anointed, ordained and instituted hierarchical power as their bishop.

Like a father he would rather have his children obey him out of love but as a father he is also ready to use his authority if needs be. The fact is that even when we do not agree with our leaders we still owe them filial obedience (Romans, chapter 13).

> *7Do ye look on things after the outward appearance? If any man trust to himself that he is Christ's, let him of himself think this again, that, as he is Christ's, even so are we Christ's. 8For though I should boast somewhat more of our authority, which the Lord hath given us for edification, and not for your destruction, I should not be ashamed: 9That I may not seem as if I would terrify you by letters. 10For his letters, say they, are weighty and powerful; but his bodily presence is weak, and his speech contemptible. 11Let such an one think this, that, such as we are in word by letters when we are absent, such will we be also in deed when we are present. 12For we dare not make ourselves of the number, or compare ourselves with some that commend themselves: but they measuring themselves by themselves, and comparing themselves among themselves, are not wise.*

Don't look at things from their outside appearance. Those who think they are in Christ let them know that I am in Christ also. This whole passage reminds us of what St. Paul said to the Corinthians in his First Letter, chapters 2 and 4. He is being very clear about his authority given him by Christ but this authority is for their encouragement not for their destruction. He is being forceful but he does not want to frighten them. On the other hand, even if they think he sounds tough in his letters and weak in his speech, he wants those who oppose him to know that what he is in his letters he is also in real life.

> *13But we will not boast of things without our measure, but according to the measure of the rule which God hath distributed to us, a measure to reach even unto you. 14For we stretch not ourselves beyond our measure, as though we reached not unto you: for we are come as far as to you also in preaching the gospel of Christ: 15Not boasting of things without our measure, that is, of other men's labours; but having hope, when your faith is increased, that we shall be enlarged by you according to our rule abundantly, 16To preach the gospel in the regions beyond you, and not to boast in another man's line of things made ready to our hand. 17But he that glorieth, let him glory in the Lord. 18For not he that commendeth himself is approved, but whom the Lord commendeth.*

This is no boasting or pride. This is only the truth. St. Paul will not go beyond the power that God has given him. But he will go to the full extent of that power to reach them. He has reached the Corinthians through the preaching of the Gospel. St. Paul will not go beyond his authority and benefit of someone else's labor. He hopes that as their faith increases, his influence among them will increase also that he may move on and go preach the Gospel to others. His pride is in the Lord because the only approval he needs is the Lord's approval. As St. Paul explains the limits of his authority, he also sets the boundaries that he will not tolerate others to push. He preached the Gospel to the Corinthians and therefore he has full authority over them as set by God. He will not overreach into someone else's work and he will not tolerate someone else to overreach into his work.

This is not a tyrannical exercise of authority that St. Paul is performing. This is the pride and jealousy of a father that he is showing. The Corinthians are his flock. They are his children. He is acting out of love and protection. Their faith is being attacked by a few. He will not tolerate anyone to interfere with their salvation. This is the mission given him by God.

Chapter 11

¹Would to God ye could bear with me a little in my folly: and indeed bear with me. ²For I am jealous over you with godly jealousy: for I have espoused you to one husband, that I may present you as a chaste virgin to Christ. ³But I fear, lest by any means, as the serpent beguiled Eve through his subtilty, so your minds should be corrupted from the simplicity that is in Christ. ⁴For if he that cometh preacheth another Jesus, whom we have not preached, or if ye receive another spirit, which ye have not received, or another gospel, which ye have not accepted, ye might well bear with him. ⁵For I suppose I was not a whit behind the very chiefest apostles. ⁶But though I be rude in speech, yet not in knowledge; but we have been throughly made manifest among you in all things.

I wished to God you would bear with me a little foolishness. I am jealous for you with a godly jealousy. To describe what is happening in the Corinthian church, St. Paul compares them as a bride who like Eve was deceived by the arguments of the serpent. Other leaders are leading them astray. They are preaching another gospel, another spirit, another Jesus than the one St. Paul has taught. But here they are ready to accept anything that sounds vaguely spiritual. These folks present themselves as super apostles. So is St. Paul, he might not sound as convincing as these preachers but what he knows he knows it is true and he has proven himself with the Corinthians.

At first we might wonder what is St. Paul saying when he speaks of his jealousy. Isn't jealousy condemned in the Ten

Commandments (thou shall not covet thy neighbor's wife and thou shall not covet thy neighbor's goods)?

The Ten Commandments speak of wanting something that someone else has and does not belong to us. Here St. Paul is using a meaning of the word that is very common in the Mediterranean languages. The word "jealous" here has the same meaning as the Latin and Greek word "zealous." St. Paul is zealous for the Corinthians faith and salvation. He is not jealous of them. He is zealous for them. He is protective of them and he will defend them against all spiritual attacks. In this sense it is a strong stand that he is taking, the stand of a wolf protecting his cubs against the attacks of the enemy preaching a different gospel.

> *7Have I committed an offence in abasing myself that ye might be exalted, because I have preached to you the gospel of God freely? 8I robbed other churches, taking wages of them, to do you service. 9And when I was present with you, and wanted, I was chargeable to no man: for that which was lacking to me the brethren which came from Macedonia supplied: and in all things I have kept myself from being burdensome unto you, and so will I keep myself. 10As the truth of Christ is in me, no man shall stop me of this boasting in the regions of Achaia. 11Wherefore? because I love you not? God knoweth.*

What did I do to you? Was I being too nice when preaching the Gospel free of charge? Did I steal money from other churches when you needed it? Instead when I was with you I did not burden anyone because those brothers who came down from Macedonia took care of my needs. Why did I do that? Because, as God knows, I love you.

> *12But what I do, that I will do, that I may cut off occasion from them which desire occasion; that wherein they glory, they may be found even as we. 13For such are false apostles, deceitful workers, transforming themselves into*

the apostles of Christ. [14]And no marvel; for Satan himself is transformed into an angel of light. [15]Therefore it is no great thing if his ministers also be transformed as the ministers of righteousness; whose end shall be according to their works.

I will keep doing what I have been doing in order to eliminate any occasion to complain for those who like to complain and compare themselves to us. These are false apostles who pretend to be apostles of Christ. No wonder, they are like Satan who disguises himself as an angel of light. No wonder that his followers do the same. Their end will be according to their works.

St. Paul is using the strongest language possible against those who teach heresy or teach relative morality. The problem in the Corinthian Church according to the first letter was that some leaders accepted incest and other types of immorality in the church as if this had no impact on their salvation. They also had a sacrilegious attitude toward Communion. At every turn St. Paul had to remind them that God punished the Hebrews (1 Cor 10:2-5), that he will destroy the Corinthians even if they are the Temple of the Holy Spirit (1 Cor 3:16-17) and that they are drinking damnation on themselves (1 Cor 11:29).

Nothing seems to have changed and he is condemning divisions and immorality as actions that will bring those leaders to hell. Actions impact salvation and St. Paul does not take heresy and schism kindly.

[16]I say again, Let no man think me a fool; if otherwise, yet as a fool receive me, that I may boast myself a little. [17]That which I speak, I speak it not after the Lord, but as it were foolishly, in this confidence of boasting. [18]Seeing that many glory after the flesh, I will glory also. [19]For ye suffer fools gladly, seeing ye yourselves are wise. [20]For ye suffer, if a man bring you into bondage, if a man devour you, if a man take of you, if a man exalt himself, if a man smite you on

the face.

St. Paul raises the tone. Don't take me for a fool. Even if you do, then let me be a fool and boast. After all you accept fools who put you in bondage and take advantage of you. Let me be a fool as well and bear with me.

> *²¹I speak as concerning reproach, as though we had been weak. Howbeit whereinsoever any is bold, (I speak foolishly,) I am bold also. ²²Are they Hebrews? so am I. Are they Israelites? so am I. Are they the seed of Abraham? so am I. ²³Are they ministers of Christ? (I speak as a fool) I am more; in labours more abundant, in stripes above measure, in prisons more frequent, in deaths oft. ²⁴Of the Jews five times received I forty stripes save one. ²⁵Thrice was I beaten with rods, once was I stoned, thrice I suffered shipwreck, a night and a day I have been in the deep; ²⁶In journeyings often, in perils of waters, in perils of robbers, in perils by mine own countrymen, in perils by the heathen, in perils in the city, in perils in the wilderness, in perils in the sea, in perils among false brethren; ²⁷In weariness and painfulness, in watchings often, in hunger and thirst, in fastings often, in cold and nakedness. ²⁸Beside those things that are without, that which cometh upon me daily, the care of all the churches. ²⁹Who is weak, and I am not weak? who is offended, and I burn not?*

If St. Paul has anything to be sorry about, it is to have been too lenient with these people. If they boast to be Jews, so is he. They pretend to be ministers of Christ, but he is a minister but even more so. St. Paul has been beaten, whipped, stoned, in prison and often near death. He has been robbed and shipwrecked. He has suffered hunger and thirst, cold and nakedness. And every day he suffers also the pressures and anxieties from all his churches.

> *³⁰If I must needs glory, I will glory of the things which concern mine infirmities. ³¹The God and Father of our Lord*

Jesus Christ, which is blessed for evermore, knoweth that I lie not. [32] In Damascus the governor under Aretas the king kept the city of the Damascenes with a garrison, desirous to apprehend me: [33] And through a window in a basket was I let down by the wall, and escaped his hands.

If I must boast I will boast of my weakness. God knows that I don't lie. Even in Damascus I had to flee the guards of the governor, through a window, in a basket.

This long passage shows St. Paul upset by the way he is treated by some people in the Church. It's not so much anger that He has but rather frustration and hurt. At a personal level we know that we are the most hurt by those we love the most because we give them all we have. We expect to be hurt by strangers but we never expect it by those we love.

Chapter 12

¹It is not expedient for me doubtless to glory. I will come to visions and revelations of the Lord. ²I knew a man in Christ above fourteen years ago, (whether in the body, I cannot tell; or whether out of the body, I cannot tell: God knoweth;) such an one caught up to the third heaven. ³And I knew such a man, (whether in the body, or out of the body, I cannot tell: God knoweth;) ⁴How that he was caught up into paradise, and heard unspeakable words, which it is not lawful for a man to utter. ⁵Of such an one will I glory: yet of myself I will not glory, but in mine infirmities. ⁶For though I would desire to glory, I shall not be a fool; for I will say the truth: but now I forbear, lest any man should think of me above that which he seeth me to be, or that he heareth of me. ⁷And lest I should be exalted above measure through the abundance of the revelations, there was given to me a thorn in the flesh, the messenger of Satan to buffet me, lest I should be exalted above measure. ⁸For this thing I besought the Lord thrice, that it might depart from me. ⁹And he said unto me, My grace is sufficient for thee: for my strength is made perfect in weakness. Most gladly therefore will I rather glory in my infirmities, that the power of Christ may rest upon me. ¹⁰Therefore I take pleasure in infirmities, in reproaches, in necessities, in persecutions, in distresses for Christ's sake: for when I am weak, then am I strong.

St. Paul needs to boast about himself, not out of pride but because he needs to set himself apart from the false teachers in Corinth. Those false teachers in the church can say they are super apostles, but he can speak of his visions and revelations. St. Paul speaks of himself in the third person singular ("I knew a man"). He has been very intimate with his feeling during the last eleven chapters of the letter. Now he is going to relate a fact that might seem too incredible. He has had a vision of heaven. The use of the third person allows him to recount his experience not just as a personal revelation but as an objective fact. He knows he has been to paradise in the presence of God but he cannot explain it. Was it a physical experience or an out of body experience? He does not know. He cannot utter or find the words necessary to explain it.

He could glory in that but he doesn't want anyone to think of him more than he is. He could boast of his experience but to prevent him to do so God has given him a thorn on his side to put him back in his place and humble him. Many times he asked the Lord to take that thorn away from him but God's answer is always "my grace is sufficient for you." In St. Paul's theology infirmities and persecutions are a source for glory because it is in these that we see Christ's power.

We don't know what St. Paul's "thorn on the side" is. It might be an illness or an emotional distress. As the two letters to the Corinthians point to false teachers in the church, these might be the people he is referring to. In any case the point is that he is persevering through the physical and spiritual battles of his ministry.

It is also a great teaching point for us. We all have had the experience of being rejected by those we love, spouses, children, parents. We might have had a death in the family or lost a job or gone through bankruptcy or any other distress that pushes us to the limits of evil in our lives. We might be a laborer who barely makes minimum wage or we might live in a country where we are persecuted, our churches burned and our families killed. We might have cancer or just survived a deadly car accident. All of these things do matter. Blessings or sufferings cannot be minimized. We cannot disregard them.

On the other hand we must remember that God is in charge, not us. Even when we don't see a reason for God allowing this or that situation in our life we can always learn from it what he wants us to learn from it. God brings good out of evil and eventually all of this is for our sanctification and salvation. No matter how humanly hard it is we must always trust in God. His grace is sufficient for us.

> [11]*I am become a fool in glorying; ye have compelled me: for I ought to have been commended of you: for in nothing am I behind the very chiefest apostles, though I be nothing.* [12]*Truly the signs of an apostle were wrought among you in all patience, in signs, and wonders, and mighty deeds.* [13]*For what is it wherein ye were inferior to other churches, except it be that I myself was not burdensome to you? forgive me this wrong.*

St. Paul should not have had to boast about himself. The Corinthians should have done it because they know all that St. Paul has done for them. The true signs of an apostle are his patience, and the spiritual works he does. The only thing that they lack from him is that he has never been a burden to them.

> [14]*Behold, the third time I am ready to come to you; and I will not be burdensome to you: for I seek not yours, but you: for the children ought not to lay up for the parents, but the parents for the children.* [15]*And I will very gladly spend and be spent for you; though the more abundantly I love you, the less I be loved.* [16]*But be it so, I did not burden you: nevertheless, being crafty, I caught you with guile.* [17]*Did I make a gain of you by any of them whom I sent unto you?* [18]*I desired Titus, and with him I sent a brother. Did Titus make a gain of you? walked we not in the same spirit? walked we not in the same steps?*

Next time St. Paul will visit the Corinthians he will not be a burden to them either. He is not after their money. The only thing he wants from them is themselves. He will gladly exhaust himself for them even though he knows that the more he loves them and the less they love him. He did not take advantage of them, neither did Titus or anyone else he has sent.

> *¹⁹Again, think ye that we excuse ourselves unto you? we speak before God in Christ: but we do all things, dearly beloved, for your edifying. ²⁰For I fear, lest, when I come, I shall not find you such as I would, and that I shall be found unto you such as ye would not: lest there be debates, envyings, wraths, strifes, backbitings, whisperings, swellings, tumults: ²¹And lest, when I come again, my God will humble me among you, and that I shall bewail many which have sinned already, and have not repented of the uncleanness and fornication and lasciviousness which they have committed.*

All of what St. Paul has said is not to defend himself. He has only been speaking the truth for the Corinthians' sake and with God as his witness. By doing so, he is trying to avoid infighting, anger, back stabbing, gossip and disorder. He is giving them advance notice so that, when he comes, he doesn't have to mourn those who have not repented of their immoral lives.

Chapter 13

¹This is the third time I am coming to you. In the mouth of two or three witnesses shall every word be established. ²I told you before, and foretell you, as if I were present, the second time; and being absent now I write to them which heretofore have sinned, and to all other, that, if I come again, I will not spare: ³Since ye seek a proof of Christ speaking in me, which to you-ward is not weak, but is mighty in you. ⁴For though he was crucified through weakness, yet he liveth by the power of God. For we also are weak in him, but we shall live with him by the power of God toward you.

This is the third time St. Paul is going to Corinth. He will make sure every fact finding will be based on two or three witnesses. This verse seems somehow out of place until we remember that the language comes from Deuteronomy 17:1-7. St. Paul is in fact considering as idolatry whatever has been committed by some of the Corinthians, whether it is inciting division or pursuing fornication or other sins. He is talking of establishing a religious tribunal where he will judge these people on the basis of two or three witnesses (Deut. 17:6). The Mosaic law speaks of a death sentence for those sins. St. Paul is not going to apply any capital punishment but he will certainly apply excommunication for those who are found guilty (1 Corinthians 5:5).

This is the third warning he is giving. If he comes he will not spare the sinners. If the Corinthians need proof, all they need to know is that, as Christ was crucified in weakness he now lives in the power of God. And he, St. Paul, will use that same power of

God to deal with them.

St. Paul is comparing himself with Christ, his weakness is the weakness of Christ, and his power is the power of God. Often in our culture we want to reduce Christ down to his love and mercy and forgiveness toward sinners and use this as an excuse to indulge our sins. Yes, Christ forgives sinners (John 8:11); yes, he did not come to condemn the world but to save it (John 3:17). But let's not forget that Jesus, the Word, the Second Person of the Trinity, is the same God in the Old Testament and in the book of the Apocalypse. Let's not be deceived, God will not be mocked (Galatians 6:7-9). Divisions, accusations, slander are all the works of the devil. St. Paul is not going to allow this in his Church.

> *5Examine yourselves, whether ye be in the faith; prove your own selves. Know ye not your own selves, how that Jesus Christ is in you, except ye be reprobates? 6But I trust that ye shall know that we are not reprobates. 7Now I pray to God that ye do no evil; not that we should appear approved, but that ye should do that which is honest, though we be as reprobates. 8For we can do nothing against the truth, but for the truth. 9For we are glad, when we are weak, and ye are strong: and this also we wish, even your perfection. 10Therefore I write these things being absent, lest being present I should use sharpness, according to the power which the Lord hath given me to edification, and not to destruction.*

St. Paul says: examine yourselves whether you are really living the faith and that Christ is in you. I pray that you do no evil not because it would justify what we are saying but because we want you to do what is right. The truth is that we are happy when you are strong and grow in the faith. I don't want to use my God given authority because he gave it to me to build you up not to tear you down.

There is a misunderstanding among Christians that good works are only an expression of the faith that we have already received. There is a sense that this is true but this is not the language that scripture uses. Here St. Paul speaks of having a living faith. He is speaking to people who have already received the faith but are not living it. Living the faith is not something incidental to salvation that comes automatically. No, it comes by practicing it daily.

St. Paul is asking the Corinthians to do what Catholics call an examination of conscience. Yes, good deeds will not bring us to salvation. But on the other hand, evil deeds will bring us to damnation. These few verses give us the same warning that St. John gives in his first letter (1 John 1:5-10). St. Paul is reminding the Corinthians to examine their faith and repent.

> ¹¹*Finally, brethren, farewell. Be perfect, be of good comfort, be of one mind, live in peace; and the God of love and peace shall be with you. ¹²Greet one another with an holy kiss.¹³All the saints salute you. ¹⁴The grace of the Lord Jesus Christ, and the love of God, and the communion of the Holy Ghost, be with you all. Amen.*

This is the closing greeting of St. Paul "*Be perfect, be of good comfort, be of one mind, live in peace; and the God of love and peace shall be with you.*" Somehow we are left with the feeling that St. Paul has to remind the Corinthians how to live the Christian life because they are not living it. These things are what God wants from us. The Christian life is not incidental to the faith it is the faith, the love of God and the love of neighbor go hand in hand (1 John 4:20). We cannot love God if we don't love our neighbor.

If we are not living a godly life or we lack spiritual comfort or we fail to bring comfort to others, if we cannot find unity in ourselves or in our families, if we do not have peace in our heart or with our spouses, children, parents or coworkers, then we know the devil is working in our lives and we are letting him. Therefore be perfect, of good comfort, of one mind, and live in peace. Live the

Christian life and the God of love and peace shall be with you.

Reflections on the Themes

Giuseppe Scillia

Christians hurting Christians

The Corinthians have hurt St. Paul deeply. These are his children but their actions, their attitude, their rejection has caused him deep pain. In the First Letter to the Corinthians, St. Paul takes a theological approach. Being saved does not mean you can do anything you want. Remember how God punished the Hebrews in the desert (1 Cor. 10:5), this is a warning to us that he will punish us just as strongly (1 Cor. 10:6). Sexual immorality will bring us damnation (1 Cor. 6:9-10) so will the disrespect of the Eucharist (1 Cor.11:27-29). Obey your elders (1 Cor. 13:17). Divisions are the work of the devil. The word itself comes from the Greek meaning "the one who divides" or "the one who slanders."

St. Paul has been slandered and bad-mouthed by the Corinthians (2 Cor. 6:8). In this Second Letter divisions still exists, sexual immorality is still prevalent but now St. Paul is looking for mutual comfort (chapter 1:4), forgiveness (chapter 2:10) and reconciliation (chapter 5:19). Like a father he had to be severe and cause them sorrow but it was for their own good. He regrets it at an emotional level but he does not regret it at a disciplinary level because it has brought them to repentance (chapter 7:8-10). He seeks his children's affection (chapter 6:12-13) but their love for him is lacking (chapter 12:13-15) and he is being personally attacked (chapter 11:1-15).

We are hurt mainly by those we love because we do not expect them to hurt us. Throughout the letter we have a sense of the pain St. Paul is suffering. This is not just an emotional issue, it is also a question of trust. Once trust is broken it is hard to heal. When we lose trust in someone, we lose faith in them. It takes two people to make a relationship, it takes one person to break it. This is a spiritual evil. Even those who do not believe in God can experience this as spiritual death. It is no wonder that spouses who have lost trust in each other end up in divorce experience mourning stages similar to those after the death of a loved one.

We think that just because we are good Christians we don't hurt anybody or nobody should hurt us. I am not speaking here of our secular culture. I am not speaking of the horrible persecutions that some Christians suffer day in and day out. I am not speaking of wars or genocides. I am speaking of those we love. I am speaking of a wife who ignores her husband; a husband who is a workaholic. A father who is not available to his children; a child who hates his parents. A brother who is mad about an inheritance. A fellow Christian who believes she knows better than her pastor; a pastor who dominates his staff. Churches often see more political feuds than Washington.

We have strong laws against physical abuse. You cannot spank a child. You cannot punch a co-worker. Black marks on a child's legs or a co-worker's broken jaw will land you in jail really fast. You cannot punch your boss but he can insult you in front of the whole office and there is no law against that. Emotional pain can often hurt more than physical pain and it can last a lifetime. Spouses divorce each other, children become traumatized, siblings are estranged. Words and attitudes are more powerful than actions. *The tongue is a fire, a world of iniquity: so is the tongue among our members, that it defileth the whole body, and setteth on fire the course of nature; and it is set on fire of hell.*" (James 3:6). The tongue that a wife uses to sting, the tongue that a husband uses to insult, the tongue that a father uses to belittle, they all come from hell.

As Christians we have the tendency to think that we should be spared pain and hurt because we are saved and we have faith. We think that the life of grace means that nothing will happen to us. We claim that being saved means we can sin and still be forgiven.

We judge others people's actions and condemn them. Not so says St. James (James 3:1), the tongue is a restless evil (James 3:8). Because we think we live under grace we cannot do anything wrong and forget St. John's warning that if we say we have no sin we are liars (1 John 1:8). The key to avoid our own conceit is confession. Not confession as psychological therapy, but confession as sacramental help (1 John 1:9).

This sin, this hurt, this suffering is true in the whole history of salvation from the day Adam broke trust with God, down to our own personal individual experiences. Divisions between spouses and among siblings, divisions in the parish and divisions in the Church are great evils. St. Paul has experienced attacks against his authority as the bishop of his congregation, as well as against him personally. This, of course, is not a rejection by every single Corinthian. It is rather a rejection by a few vocal and influential individuals (chapter 11:5). No matter how small, divisions harm individuals but ultimately they harm the Body of Christ.

Mercy and Glory

For we preach not ourselves, but Christ Jesus the Lord; and ourselves your servants for Jesus' sake. For God, who commanded the light to shine out of darkness, hath shined in our hearts, to give the light of the knowledge of the glory of God in the face of Jesus Christ. (Chapter 4:5-6)

What is the Glory of God? St. Paul tells us that Jesus gives us the light to know the glory of God. When we consult the dictionary it tells us that "glory" means praise, honor majesty, fame, beauty, splendor, thanksgiving. In a short verse St. Paul tells us that Jesus is the praise, honor, majesty, fame, beauty, splendor and thanksgiving of God. In praising Christ we give thanks to God. In seeing Jesus, we see the majesty of God, his beauty and his splendor.

We preach Christ Jesus as Lord, the way, the truth and the life (John 14:6), says St. Paul. He is also the light of the world (John 8:12) that shines in darkness (John 1:5). That light is the knowledge of the glory of God (chapter 4:6). Jesus Christ is the light, the glory, the knowledge of God the Father (John 14:7). Jesus is the physical manifestation of God and in him we see who God is. In contemplating the face of Jesus, we know and understand God. God is love. Jesus is the personification of that love. Since the beginning of creation, at the fall of Adam and Eve, when God cursed the serpent he also promised Adam and Eve a savior (Genesis 3:15). Since the beginning, at the fall of Adam and Eve, God already showed his love and mercy. Jesus is that love and mercy. Like Father, like Son.

In his proclamation of the Year of Mercy, Pope Francis says:

Jesus Christ is the face of the Father's mercy. These words might well sum up the mystery of the Christian faith. Mercy has become living and visible in Jesus of Nazareth, reaching its culmination in him. The Father, "rich in mercy" (Ephesians 2:4) [...] sent his only Son into the world, born of the Virgin Mary, to reveal his love for us in a definitive way. Whoever sees Jesus sees the Father (John 14:9). Jesus of Nazareth, by his words, his actions, and his entire person reveals the mercy of God.

The mercy of God the Father is seen in Jesus' incarnation. In the Gospel of John, chapter 1:1-14, Jesus is seen as the Logos of God, the reason and wisdom of God, who came to witness the light of God, his mercy and salvation. He created the whole cosmos (*"all things were made by him"* – John 1:3) for one thing and one thing only to dwell among us (*"dwelt among us and we beheld his glory"* – John 1:14).

We see the glory of God in his creation (psalm 19:1). We can know the invisible God in his creation (Romans 1:19-20). Creation has a beginning, middle and an end. It is a story with a purpose and a goal. Christ is that purpose and that goal. From the beginning the purpose of God was not to be praised for his glory but to share it with us. Humans are the perfection of creation, created in the image of God (Genesis 1-27) and God's desire is to live with us humans. He walks with Adam (Genesis 3:8) and dwells with us (John 1:14). God dwells in the tabernacle and the temple of Israel where the cloud of the glory of God filled the Holy of Holies (Exodus 40:34-35 and 1 Kings 8:10-11). When we search the www.JewishEncyclopedia.com the link for "Glory of God" is the word "Shekinah." It is defined as *"the majestic presence or manifestation of God which has descended to "dwell" among men."*

What St. Paul is saying (chapter 4:6) is: the knowledge of the glory and majesty of God is seen in Jesus Christ who is the Shekinah Glory, the love and mercy of God through the presence of Jesus Christ among his people, in a real way. This is what we, Christians, should preach, not ourselves (chapter 4:5) but God's love and presence among us, in a real way. We, Catholics, know and live this in the Eucharist, God with us, Emmanuel (Matthew 1:23).

Be Reconciled with God

Therefore if any man be in Christ, he is a new creature: old things are passed away; behold, all things are become new. And all things are of God, who hath reconciled us to himself by Jesus Christ, and hath given to us the ministry of reconciliation; To wit, that God was in Christ, reconciling the world unto himself, not imputing their trespasses unto them; and hath committed unto us the word of reconciliation. Now then we are ambassadors for Christ, as though God did beseech you by us: we pray you in Christ's stead, be ye reconciled to God. (Chapter 5:17-20)

These few verses are dense with doctrine and theology. When St. Paul was saved, it was by Jesus Christ that he was reconciled with God who gave him the ministry of reconciliation. As Catholics, we know that when St. Paul speaks of the ministry of reconciliation he is speaking of forgiveness of sins through sacramental confession. We know this because Jesus gave the apostles the power to bind and loose (Matthew 18:18) in the context of the apostles being able to judge disputes among believers as a judiciary body, the Church (Matthew 18:18). Judging disputes among believers means that there must be some leaders who are anointed for this role. Not all believers can have the power to judge other believers or their judgments would be biased. Let's use the example of a divorce. There are disputes, there is possibly sin involved. Which spouse can be the judge? Which spouse's judgment remains binding on earth and in heaven? Yes, a spouse can forgive the other and let go of all bitterness but he or she cannot make final judgment on someone else's true reconciliation or the eternal destiny of their soul. The whole example even falls apart because Jesus does not allow divorce (Mark 10:9-12). Who is then allowed to judge disputes and minister reconciliation? This power to bind and loose even in heaven can only given to a few by the power of the Holy Spirit.

According to John this is exactly what happened on the Sunday after Easter when Jesus gives the Holy Spirit to the apostles to forgive sins (John 20:19-23). St. Paul only repeats what Jesus has already said. It is because Jesus was sent by the Father to reconcile the world (John 20:21) that St. Paul has received this ministry of reconciliation (chapter 5:18). As priests, the primary role of the Apostles is to preach the forgiveness of sins and offer sacrifice, that it is to administer Confession and offer the Eucharist.

Some Christians think this power to bind and loose apply to all believers and give these verses a psychological meaning. Sure there is a certain sense that if I forgive others I will be forgiven and find peace but there is no way that by forgiving or not forgiving others my decision can bind them or loose them in heaven or otherwise. If the ministry of reconciliation was a ministry for all believers then it would include the Corinthians as well but St. Paul is not including them as he is begging them to be reconciled to God. The Corinthians are Christians but their divisions and sins have taken them away from grace and St. Paul is begging them to come back to obedience and reconciliation through his ministry.

This is not the repentance and reconciliation that we first experience when we first believe and are baptized (Mark 16:16). The Corinthians are already Christians therefore St. Paul is speaking of the ongoing repentance and reconciliation we must always seek throughout our lives because at the last judgment what we do in our lives will have eternal consequences (Chapter 5:10).

This in no way is a psychological, feel good, calling to forgive others. It certainly can be understood that all Christians, by their witness, can bring others to Christ. We all have the calling for the Great Commission but we do not have the sacramental ministry to administer reconciliation (Chapter 5:18), only priests have the ministry and power to forgive sins. We know that only God can forgive sins but we also know he has given this power to men (Matthew 9:6-8; Luke and Mark's parallels). It is this same power that Jesus conveys to the Apostles (John 20:21) through the Holy Spirit: to forgive sins in order to reconcile us to God (John 20:22-23).

We know that redemption, justification, sanctification and salvation, have only one purpose: to reconcile us with God (Colossians 1:20). This ultimate reconciliation culminates in a new life with God, in the beatific vision therefore be reconciled with God.

Handing Down the Faith

But I fear, lest by any means, as the serpent beguiled Eve through his subtilty, so your minds should be corrupted from the simplicity that is in Christ. For if he that cometh preacheth another Jesus, whom we have not preached, or if ye receive another spirit, which ye have not received, or another gospel, which ye have not accepted, ye might well bear with him. (Chapter 11:3-4)

Fidelity to the faith handed down by the Apostles is important to St. Paul. He brings it up to the Galatians by cursing those who teach another Gospel (Galatians 1:6-9). Here he calls those who preach another doctrine as being the deceiving serpent of Genesis, Satan (chapter 11:3-4). I was listening to a radio broadcast by a pastor in the Philadelphia area who boasted that he knew that the doctrine of the Rapture is something new in the history of the Church but because it is in the Bible it is true and he will believe it. It did not occur to him why other Christians in previous centuries never taught this. When a preacher says he is teaching something that was taught before it should bring anyone to pause. It brings a false dichotomy between the scripture and the Church historical teachings as if Scripture and Church were somehow two opposing ideas.

There are several fallacies in these and similar comments. It is very unlikely that a 21 century American preacher may understand the Bible better than a first or second century Christian like Clement of Rome, Ignatius of Antioch or Justin Martyr. This kind of thinking leads directly to heresy. The historical continuity of the teachings of the Church from the first century to today is a guaranty that our faith is the true faith that was transmitted from Christ and his Apostles. The true measure of whether this church or that church is teaching the true Christian faith is whether its teachings are the same as the teachings the Church taught at the beginning (1 Timothy 3:15).

To St. Paul it means that he was taught the faith by Ananias (Acts 9:19), was introduced to the Apostles by Barnabas (Acts 9:27), presented his teachings to the leaders in Jerusalem (Galatians 2:2), and was approved by St. Peter, St. John and St. James (Galatians 2:9). Even though he had direct revelations from Christ he knew he had to seek spiritual guidance and approval (anointing/ordination) from the Apostles. There is only one Gospel. The one that Jesus taught, the one that St. Peter proclaimed and the one that St. Paul preached are one and the same. The one that St. Paul handed down to the Corinthians and the one that is being preached today are one and the same. Anyone who teaches a different faith other than the one the Church taught in the beginning is doing the work of the devil, whether they are those false teachers in Corinth or other preachers in our times. The Church is the warrantor of the continuity of the faith (1 Timothy 3:15, Matthew 18:18, Matthew 19:28, Luke 22:31, John 21:15, John 21:17, 1 Corinthians 6:2-3). To me, if we want to know which church is the true Church, we have to ask which one has existed for the last 2000 years and still teaches the same doctrines it taught 2000 years ago.

This is why St. Paul compares these teachers to Satan who deceived Eve (chapter 11:3). This is why he draws the line in the sand. Nobody, no matter how smart or convincing or charismatic he is, has any right to teach anything else than what St. Paul first taught the Corinthians. He will fight for this like a wolf protecting his cubs.

Conclusion

Divisions among Christians are harmful to the Church. All Christians agree with this statement. Why then, are there so many divisions? People, for example, disagree about the kind of music should be played for worship. It can create bad feelings among believers but it is not worthy of breaking covenantal trust with Christ and his body. These kind of divisions would not merit St. Paul comparing people who create divisions as agents of Satan (chapter 11:13-14). He is speaking of the deeper moral and doctrinal divisions. There can be unity even if the 9 o'clock service has traditional music and the 10 o'clock service has country music. But there cannot be unity if one church accepts gay pastors and another does not, or one teaches contraception is permissible and another does not, or one baptizes infants and another does not.

Even when speaking of apostasy and schism, I am not sure how this can be understood when the diversity of denominations and non-denominational denominations is still accepted as a matter of fact. I have seen Pope Francis' call to Christian unity being decried as a call for a one world religion. In our twenty first century America, the church is seen as a federation rather than a kingdom and the fear of a one world religion is fueled by a misunderstanding of Revelation 13:12. Jesus does ask for a one world kingdom and religion (Matthew 28:18, Mark 16:15, and Acts 1:8). He also prayed for a unity among believers that would be as strong as the unity that exists in the Trinity (John 17:20-25).

This call for unity that Jesus made is not a call to a loosely connected federation of self governing entities that may or may not believe in the same moral and doctrinal faith. It is a call to a unity that is inseparable from the Trinity and as a visible governing body (Matthew 18:17). When St. Paul speaks of the Church as being a body made out of different parts he is not speaking of loosely connected parts like the Lutherans and the Baptists who have opposing doctrines on infant baptism or ordination of women and homosexuals.

The Church is not a federation of self-governing body parts. This would be a comical oxymoron. St. Paul would not be using a nonsensical metaphor. On the contrary, he is speaking of organically connected parts that work together for a common good (1 Cor. 12:12-27), with the Apostles and their successors at the head of the Church (1 Cor. 12:28).

Schism and heresy are great evils. It is also a great evil when a group leaves a church because of disagreement about practice or discipline and other likes and dislikes. Divisions in the Body of Christ ultimately hurts Christ and Christianity (John 17:21).

18383339R00044

Printed in Great Britain
by Amazon